Very Important
Adult
Work, Totally Not a
Coloring Book

Geometric

ISBN 978-1-939169-05-1

Printed in the United States of America

Relax with Pleasing Patterns

What is it about geometric shapes and repeated patterns that makes them so soothing? There's nothing more satisfying than coloring intricate combinations of looping spirals, solid squares, and bright diamonds.

Patterned coloring pages don't have a larger concept to hem you in. You can tease out your own comprehensive picture based on color combinations and imagination. This book has limitless possibilities for adults in touch with their creativity.

The patterns on these pages range from wide and simple lines to tiny, detailed designs. Watch them come to life with any coloring tool—crayons, colored pencils, paint, or markers.

It's time to relax and tap into your meditative, artistic side. Geometric shapes and configurations are everywhere, just waiting for you to apply your own personal flair.

✧✧✧

Also available for your coloring pleasure:

Floral Coloring Pages, ISBN 978-1-939169-03-7
Mandala Coloring Pages, ISBN 978-1-939169-04-4

Visit

www.AdultColoringPages.net

for more coloring goodness

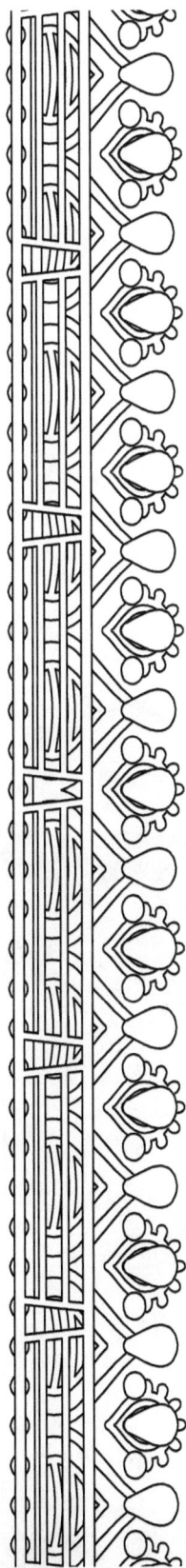

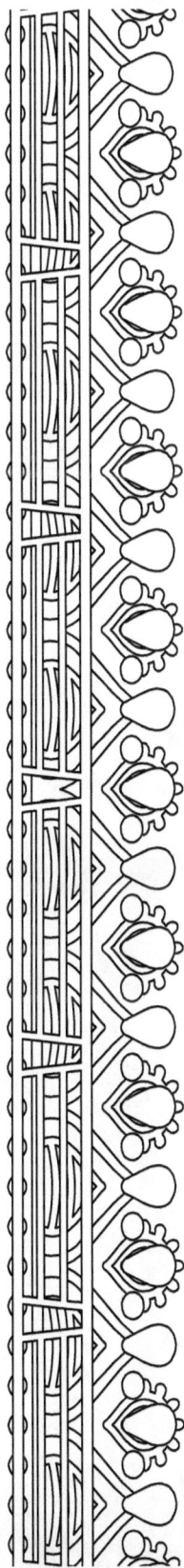

Visit

www.AdultColoringPages.net

for more coloring goodness

Visit

www.AdultColoringPages.net

for more coloring goodness

Visit

www.AdultColoringPages.net

for more coloring goodness

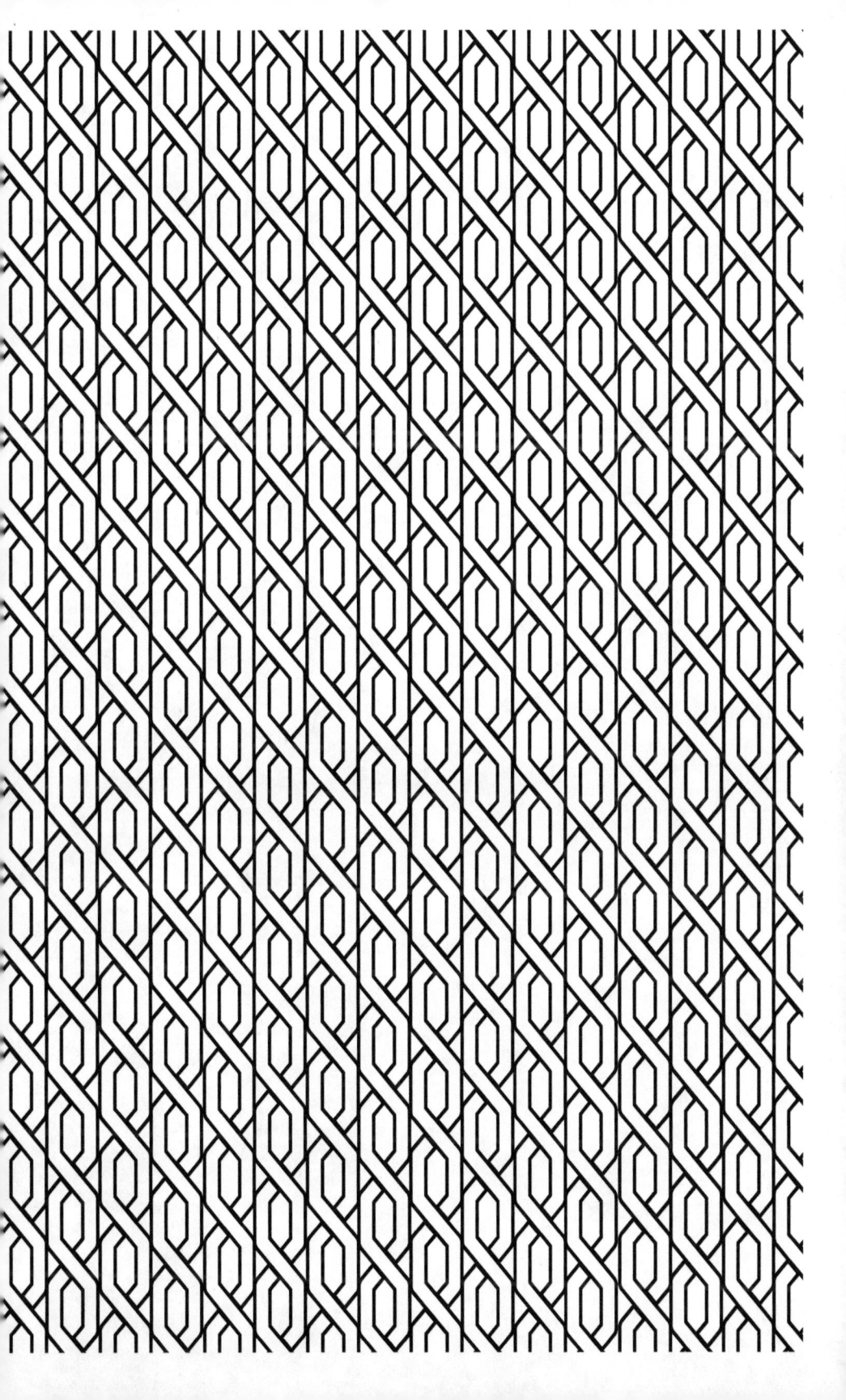

Visit

www.AdultColoringPages.net

for more coloring goodness

Visit

www.AdultColoringPages.net

for more coloring goodness

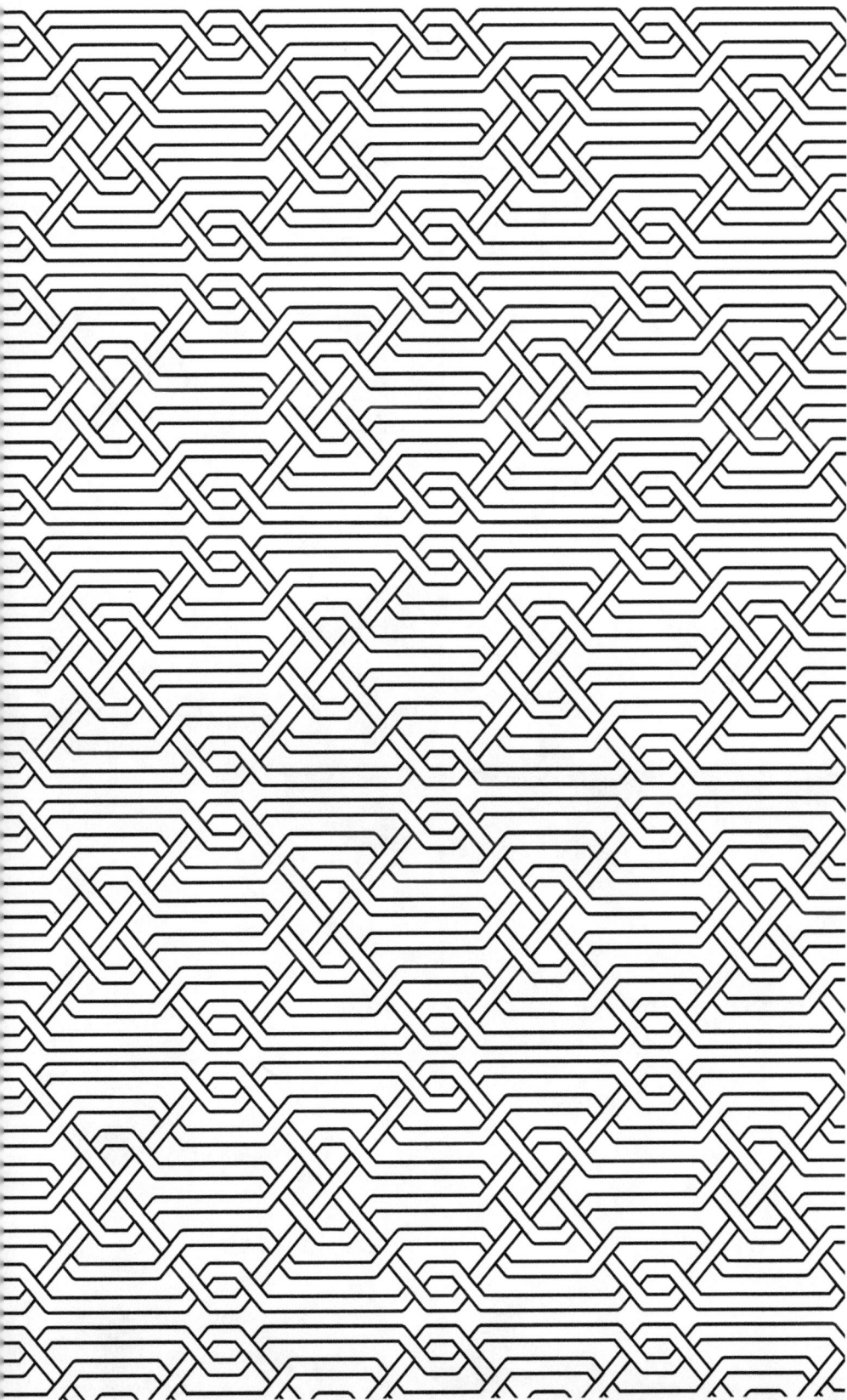

Visit

www.AdultColoringPages.net

for more coloring goodness

Visit

www.AdultColoringPages.net

for more coloring goodness

Visit

www.AdultColoringPages.net

for more coloring goodness

Visit

www.AdultColoringPages.net

for more coloring goodness

Visit

www.AdultColoringPages.net

for more coloring goodness

Also Available for Your Coloring Pleasure:

Floral Coloring Pages, ISBN 978-1-939169-03-7

Mandala Coloring Pages, ISBN 978-1-939169-04-4

www.ingramcontent.com/pod-product-compliance
Lightning Source LLC
Chambersburg PA
CBHW070816050426
42452CB00011B/2073